A WORKING LIFE ON THE GREA

A PORTRAIT OF A CAMBRIDGESHIRE FEN FAMILY

NITA LUXFORD

S.B. Publications

DEDICATION

This book is dedicated to the memory of Thomas Arthur and Mary Ann Metcalfe, Dolly Arnold, Tom and Alma Arnold, and is for twins Olive Parr and Jack Arnold, who agreed to have their memories and family photographs recorded here. It is also for all who knew Thomas Arthur Metcalfe and those who wish to catch a glimpse of this larger than life countryman, his ancestors and descendants, and their life on the Great Ouse, Holywell.

First published in 2000 by S B Publications
19 Grove Road, Seaford, Sussex BN25 1TP
Telephone 01323 893498: Fax 01323 893860

ISBN 1 85770 208 5

Typeset by JEM Editorial – JEMedit@AOL.com

Printed and bound by MFP Design & Print
Longford Trading Estate, Thomas Street,
Stretford, Manchester
M32 0JT

CONTENTS

ACKNOWLEDGEMENTS

Thanks are due to the following, for their valuable assistance in compiling this book:
A Akeroyd and staff of the Huntingdon Record Office; B Burn-Murdoch and P Seamark of the St Ives Norris Museum; Cambridge Record Office staff; Huntingdon and St Ives Library staff; and D Anderson, P Buckland, E Carter, the late R Everitt, D Griffin, the late J Harrison, R Harrison, the late I Hogan, R Hudson, V Ibbett, F Irons, M Irons, E James, D Morgan, O Morton, J Napper, O Peters, M Petty, M Smith, Ed and Er Standen, O Swan, S Tabbitt, W Tabbitt, R Watson, I Whitmore, G Wilmer.

I am also grateful to those who, by a chance remark or by giving a snippet of information, sent the research in the right direction.

Thanks to David Lovegrove for additional sketches.

Special thanks to Philip Nixon for the initial inspiration; Val Norman for her eagle-eyed research assistance; Brian for the title and support; Mike and Roy Luxford for clerical back-up and the final copy; mentor Keith Elliott for his adroit tuition and Steve Benz for his encouragement and guidance.

Thanks to photographers the late J Slater, the late J Freeman and Philip Nixon for generously allowing the use of their photographs. To Philip Nixon for making transparencies of old photographs and to Les Goodey for computer enhancement of some of the old photographs.

Every effort has been made to trace copyright holders of photographs used in this book. Where this has failed, I apologize if I have infringed rights.

Wherever possible, facts and stories have been checked. I apologize if any inaccuracies occur in the text.

Nita Luxford

Pictures
Front cover: The Front, Holywell, painting by Robert Winter Fraser
Title page: Thomas Arthur Metcalfe in a gun punt in front of his home, Wildcroft
Back cover: River scene, painting by Gilbert Baird Fraser

FOREWORD

Tom Metcalfe Arnold was born in 1922. He was the last of his family to make his living on the Great Ouse at Holywell. He died in 1994. Tom's mother, Dolly (Dorothy) Arnold cut rushes from the river until her death in 1971. Dolly's father Thomas Arthur Metcalfe lived by the old fenman's skills. He was a rush-cutter, osier-cutter and merchant, eel hive-maker, eel-catcher, fisherman, wildfowler, punt-gunner and boatman; as were his brothers and their father before them. Women of the family have also been recorded as 'fisherwomen'.

Twins Olive Parr and Jack Arnold outside Wildcroft.

Wildcroft on the Front at Holywell was their family home. There are also records of the family living at The Back in the nineteenth century.

Jack Arnold looked after the rush-cutting business for a short time after his brother's death. Then, he taught Felicity Irons the skill of cutting and she took over the work.

Jack talked about family members who had worked on the river, and he had a unique collection of photographs of the work. The wealth of this material about a vanished way of life generated the idea of this book. Now, at the beginning of a new millennium, this task seems more poignant and compelling. Generously, Jack and his twin sister Olive have donated the photographs to the Public Records Office at Huntington.

INTRODUCTION

The East Anglian village of Holywell-cum-Needingworth, once situated in the small county of Huntingdonshire, lies on the northern bank of the Great Ouse. The market town of St Ives, famous for its medieval bridge incorporating a chapel, lies three miles to the west. The meandering Ouse at Holywell once marked the county boundary. In 1974, the area became part of Cambridgeshire. Holywell occupies an almost central position in the enlarged county with Cambridge to the south east.

Holywell's picturesque houses and ancient cottages lining The Front, were built on a high bank, facing south towards the river. The rear exits on higher ground, providing an escape from the seasonal flood water.

A brook flows south of The Front and fen and meadows stretch to the river. The Great Ouse is said to have changed to a more southerly course in the fourteenth century and much of the land was reclaimed.

A band of limestone running east from St Ives ends at Holywell. The church was built at this point, high above the river and the fen, where a beacon once burned to guide river traffic.

The spring which rises east of the church, gave Holywell its name. The water is said to have power to heal, reveal true love and drive away devils.

The well which gave Holywell its name.

The village road forms a ring and is joined by a panhandle, Millway, running south from Needingworth. The Ferry Boat Inn stands on The Front in the east, with Wildcroft a few yards to the west. The straight Millway, becomes Church Street and runs past the school, to Needingworth High Street, with its extended ribbon development. Most of Needingworth's old buildings were destroyed by fire in 1847. Near the War Memorial and the old lock-up, a road runs south-east for about a mile to the Pike and Eel Inn (Overcote) and the river.

The Ouse valley, on the south-west edge of the fen, comprises mainly fenland and clay, with rich gravel deposits, sand and loam. Sand and gravel have been worked at Holywell and clay dug for brick-making.

Church of St John the Baptist, Holywell.

The church of St John the Baptist looks down on an ancient site. Roman pottery and coins were found here. Possibly, one of a chain of Roman forts built along the Ouse valley was sited here.

There was a church recorded here in 890. The Saxon, Alfwara, daughter of Alwyn, gave Halliwell to the Ramsey monks in 1007. In 1349, the plague claimed the Rector and half the villagers. After the dissolution of the monasteries, the manor passed to the princess, who later became Queen Elizabeth I. The Dukes of Manchester were Lords of the Manor from 1628 to around 1877. The church tower is thought to have been built in 1547, using stone from Ramsey Abbey. The brick enclosure over the spring was erected in 1845 by the Reverend SB Beckwith. An arched structure, it allows the water to run across the meadows, towards the river.

Flowing from Oxfordshire in the west, the river rises in Northamptonshire. Wide and deep in Bedfordshire, it sluggishly echoes its name; navigable from Bedford to the sea, it flows via Denver sluice to the Wash, near King's Lynn.

In earlier times the river was an important trade route. Goods were shipped up river to the major fairs held at St Ives. Navigation was not always easy. Many disputes between mill owners and the owners of the navigation resulted in low water levels, neglect, silting and closed locks. The river was declared a public highway at the end of the nineteenth century and areas were set aside for pleasure boating.

Below Holywell the river passes through water meadows to Earith. Here the natural course was diverted to drain the fens. The modern agricultural landscape was once marsh, a few islands of higher ground housing the centres of population.

In the flooded fens, reeds, rushes, willows, fish, eels and wildfowl flourished. The isolated inhabitants used alcohol and opium poppy to fend off the ague and mosquito-borne malaria. Stoically they survived, walking on stilts, or punting and skating over their domain. For centuries men tried to drain the swamp. Often, the channels and dykes served to exacerbate the situation, and shrinking peat meant channels ran higher than the surrounding land. Windmills, and later engines, powered the pumps to move the water.

Today, a network of man-made rivers, drains and sluices, controlled by modern technology, protects the area. Still, in exceptional weather conditions, the "drowns" win the battle, as land reverts to mere.

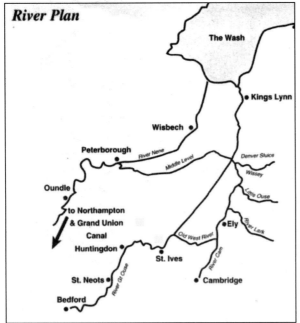

Present day navigable water of the Great Ouse.

8

The Front, Holywell. The Ferry Boat Inn is on the right behind the trees. Wildcroft and its barns are in the centre. From a painting by Robert Winter Fraser.

The Pike and Eel Inn, and ferry carrying a horse and cart, Overcote, c1900.

THE FAMILY

Dorothy Metcalfe (Dolly), an only child, married Cecil Arnold in 1919. Her son Tom was the last of the family to make a living from the Great Ouse at Holywell. He was christened Cecil Thomas Metcalfe Arnold, after his father and grandfather. The latter was fisherman and rush merchant, Thomas Arthur Metcalfe, one of a large family, living at The Front, Holywell, at the end of the nineteenth century and the beginning of the twentieth century.

By consulting the available census records, a picture of the Metcalf (Metcalfe, Medcalf) families and their links with other village families can be seen. In 1841 the population was 959 but by 1891 it had shrunk to 672, divided almost equally between the sexes.

The 1891 census records outline the area as: Holywell-cum-Needingworth, Rectory Manor, Blackey's and Spencer's Farms, Brick Kilns, Railway Gatehouse and Junction Cottages, Carpenter's Arms and Cottage on the Bluntisham Road, Over-Cote and Barges on the River Ouse lying in the Parish. This also gives an insight into the occupations and employment of the inhabitants.

A Metcalfe family lived at the Ferry Boat Inn. The first census (1841), records Thomas and Alice Metcalf (née Christmas), with daughters Jemima and Mary Ann at the inn. In 1854, Mary Ann married a lodger, brick-maker William Jackson. In 1851, the widowed Alice is logged as publican and a nephew, William (aged twenty-one), is at the inn. Mary and William Jackson are recorded in censuses from 1861 to 1891. William is described as publican and, in 1871, also a farmer, with twenty acres.

A Metcalf (Medcalf) family also lived at the Pike and Eel Inn, situated on the river bank about a mile downstream from Holywell. In 1841 the publican and farmer was John Medcalf, living with his wife Ann (nee Mehew), children James, aged twenty, Thomas, aged seventeen, and two servants. An older daughter, Rebecca, had married farmer Heard Hemmington in 1838. He came from Over, south of the river, reached by ferry from the inn. James Metcalf married Mary Thorp in 1841. Ten years later, Mary and children James and Anna Maria are recorded in Silver Street, Needingworth. By the time of the next count Mary is widowed. The 1861 records show Ann, and son Thomas, together with Ann's grandson James, aged twelve, at the Pike and Eel Inn. Records for 1871 and 1881 show Rebecca and Heard (Henry) Hemmington now in residence and by 1891 Heard's sister- n-law Mary, and her daughter Annie, aged twenty, have taken over the inn.

Thomas Metcalf, a fisherman, and his wife Elizabeth are recorded in the 1841 census living at The Front, near the Ferry Boat Inn. They had three children, William aged ten, Elizabeth aged six and Thomas, three. By 1851 they had moved to The Back and son William, now twenty-one, is recorded at the Ferry Boat Inn on census night.

In 1858, son Thomas married Emma Webster, a dressmaker, born in Upwell, and by 1861 they were living at The Front with one-year-old Emily Elizabeth. Tom's widowed mother, fisherwoman Elizabeth, and her thirteen-year-old daughter, Ann, lived next door. Over the next twenty years the family increased. The census of 1891 records Thomas as a rod and rush merchant. His three eldest sons are described as 'in the rushes'. They are Walter Webster aged twenty-nine, Thomas Arthur aged twenty-six and George aged seventeen. Fred aged fourteen and Laura, twelve, are scholars. Daughters not at home include Kate, Miriam, Ada Ann, Ellen and Emily Elizabeth. In 1876, at the age of seventeen, Emily Elizabeth married Wallis Stearn Worts, a Holywell cattle dealer. Other daughters married into the Anderson, Mitchel, Newman and Freeman families.

Looking back at the 1881 census, Kate aged seventeen, a dressmaker, is next door with her aunt, Eliza Thorpe, a farmer's wife. Kate's grandmother, Mary Ann Webster, a retired publican is also there.

Ten years earlier, Kate is logged at The Rose and Crown, Needingworth, with her aunt and uncle, Eliza and Fisher Webster. At the same time her sister Emily is recorded at Moynes Hall, a seventeenth century manor house at the east end of The Back. The householder is her aunt, Emily Thorpe. As the men died young, the surviving daughters married and the name Metcalf became less common.

At the end of the century, willow and rushes were essential materials for making furniture and all types of containers. The 1891 census describes Thomas Metcalfe as a rod and rush merchant, but he was also a fisherman and punt-gunner. Freshwater fish, including eels, were an important food source for the local people. Birds and wildfowl, rabbits and hares added variety to the winter diet.

There was enough work for three of Tom's sons to be employed 'in the rushes', although rush cutting was a summer occupation. Work dictated by the seasons, and the weather, allowed an independent way of life.

Local newspaper reports of village activities give glimpses of the family's social life. The winter of 1890-91 was very severe. In December 1890, the river at St Ives was frozen for miles.

On January 12 1891, the *Hunts County Guardian* reported that seventy-year-old William Jackson of the Ferry Boat Inn, 'respected by all who know him; his inn is a common resort of anglers during the fishing season' had accidentally broken a rib. On January 24, the paper records: 'We have now had sixty days of hard wintry weather'. The same page bears an account of 'an exciting match on the river at Holywell'. Eight Holywell-cum-Needingworth men competed against eight from Fen Drayton – the village on the south side of the river reached by ferry. Watched by a large crowd, the men skated on the frozen river and Thomas Metcalfe beat GH Johnson of Fen Drayton. Reports from other villages describe evening skating matches, lit by Chinese lanterns with brass bands playing. 13

Fenman had a long tradition of using pattens or skates to get around in winter. Skating contests were enjoyed when the land work was impossible. Bury Fen, Bluntisham, downstream from Holywell, was the scene of many international skating contests. The flooded, frozen fen, providing an excellent course. Locals also played a game known as bandy – a type of ice hockey, using a cat or ball made from wound cloth selvedges, propelled by ash sticks.

Holywell was the home of a number of artists, among them the talented Fraser family. Ardent royalists, the Frasers formed the White Cockade Jacobite Club, with the ambition of restoring the Stuart line to the throne. Meetings were held in village inns and Metcalfes were members.

The *Hunts County Guardian*, in June 1891, ran an account of a celebration of Oak Day in Holywell. On May 29 the Reverend Hoskyns allowed Mr Few to decorate the church weathercock and four pinnacles with branches of oak. The celebrations were held under the auspices of the White Cockade Jacobite Club. The Ferry Boat Inn, the club's headquarters, and the village were decorated. Visitors from the Hemingfords villages arrived in decorated conveyances and they went by ferry to Drayton drove. Here, the Hemingfords team was beaten at quoits by Thomas Metcalfe's team, which included his brother George. They all returned to Holywell for the tea served by Mrs Jackson, Miss

Mortlock and Laura Metcalfe. This was followed by a smoking concert attended by 'some hundred persons'. Fred Tabbitt gave a rendition of the Oak Apple Song and others, 'including Mr T Metcalfe, contributed to the harmony'. A full day by any standards!

The Metcalfe's house, Wildcroft, was built of brick and stands yards from the Ferry Boat Inn. Views south over the river and the flat fen provide an idyllic setting.

The rear part of Wildcroft is much older than the front. Census records and an 1887 map suggest that the site once held two households. It was thought that Tom Metcalfe's grandfather bought the house in 1750 but the relevant document is lost.

Behind the house were a stable, pigsty, storage barns and hen houses, together with a large vegetable garden. The family was virtually self-sufficient.

Thomas Metcalfe died in 1892, aged fifty-two, but his widow Emma lived to be eighty. It was their son, Thomas Arthur, who was destined to carry on the family's traditional occupations and expand them to meet the needs of the twentieth century.

Thomas Arthur's older brother, Walter Webster – well known in fishing circles – remained a bachelor. He died in 1905, aged forty-two. The Cambridge Anglers (probably a group of undergraduates) and the White Cockade Club were among those who sent flowers to his funeral.

At one time the Ouse supported a large number of otters. An amazing story appeared in the *Hunts Post* in 1908. Fred Metcalfe shot a duck at Overcote Ferry near the Pike and Eel Inn. His dog went into the river to retrieve it and was attacked by an otter. The dog was dragged under water in the middle of the river and drowned.

14

Thomas Arthur Metcalfe and dogs in front of Wildcroft.

Fred was killed while serving in the Great War. He was thirty-eight, and is one of thirteen Holywell-cum-Needingworth men recorded on the Portland stone memorial at the junction of Needingworth and Overcote roads. The memorial was unveiled at the end of 1920.

There is little information about George Metcalfe. He probably left the village at the end of the nineteenth century, and may have emigrated to Australia.

In April 1896, thirty-two-year-old Thomas Arthur married Mary Ann Jeeps in St Anne's Church, Impington. She was the twenty-eight-year-old fourth daughter of Robert and Mary Jeeps, who also had a son, Robert. Like many women at the time, Mary Ann had been in service. The 1881 census records her employed by Thomas Ellwood of Grantchester.

Mary Ann Jeeps.

Thomas Arthur's grandmother, fisherwoman Elizabeth, died in June 1896, aged seventy-seven. She did not survive to see the birth of Tom and Mary Ann's daughter. Dorothy Mary (Dolly) was baptised in Holywell church on December 6, 1896 and was to be treasured as their only child.

The following year Queen Victoria celebrated her diamond jubilee. In Holywell-cum-Needingworth, according to the *Hunts Post*, on July 22, celebrations included a cycle parade. 'The costumed cyclists, grotesque and amusing, created much merriment.' At 1pm the men and boys sat down to a substantial dinner and at 3pm, women and girls enjoyed a 'meat tea'. The next day every family received bread and meat, old men were given 2s 6d and old ladies 2s. All men aged sixty and over were included in a draw for agricultural implements; for women, there was a draw for drapery. Sports were held in a field belonging to a Mr Sandifer and prizes were presented by the Reverend Cecil Northgate, son of the Rector.

In 1900, the year before Queen Victoria's death, the navigation disputes on the Great Ouse were finally over and the lock gates were opened. The Metcalfes took advantage of the increased pleasure boating on the river and the demand for overnight accommodation. Wildcroft became a guest house and Tom Metcalfe (Thomas Arthur) hired out punts to fishermen.

Dolly Metcalfe grew to be an accomplished horsewoman, which was to prove invaluable in her later life. Musical, she sang and played the piano, and acted as church organist for several years.

Mary Ann was straight-laced and a strict parent, while Tom Metcalfe taught Dolly about the natural world on which their livelihood centred and depended. As a result of mixing with guests from across the social strata, Dolly became confident in any company.

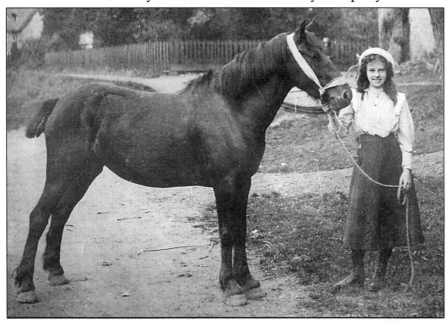

Dolly Metcalfe with her horse Kitty.

The building seen behind Dolly in this picture is the fisherman's barn. Across the road, the picket-fenced orchard supplied plums, pears and apples for the family. Reed cottage, next to the orchard, was home to artist Gilbert Baird Fraser and his wife, who ran a small school. The Anchor Inn, haunt of watermen, stood alongside and next was Brooklyn, the house given by Tom Metcalfe to Dolly, on her twenty-first birthday. Her neighbours, the Tabbitt family, lived in Oak Cottage, out of view.

Growing into an attractive young woman, Dolly met a young policeman, John Henry Cecil Arnold. He came from

Farcet near Peterborough, not far from the area where the great Whittlesey Mere once flowed. Drained in 1850, it was a vast lake teeming with wildlife of all descriptions – the scene of wild fowling, fishing, pleasure boating and winter skating.

During the 1914-18 War the territorial battalions of the Huntingdonshire Cyclists were formed to support the regular Army. The photograph below shows Cecil Arnold in what is thought to be the Cyclists' uniform. Unfortunately, it bears no identifying badges, and the battalions' records are incomplete. The portrait is on a *card postale* that bears a message to Cecil's father. It is written on the back in indelible pencil, but the card was not stamped and was probably enclosed in a letter.

Dolly at seventeen.

17

Cecil married Dolly after the war, and after leaving the police force. The wedding on December 18, 1919, at St John's Church, was a big event for the village of Holywell. A detailed account appeared in the *Hunts Post*.

The couple were married by the Rector, the Reverend JA Ross, at a choral service. Dolly wore a grey costume with a powder blue hat, and her bridesmaid was Cecil's sister Lily. Many guests attended the reception at Wildcroft, including, from London, Sir Henry and Lady Dallrymple, Mr Amor and Mr and Mrs Leman.

Cecil gave Dolly a diamond ring and she gave him the gift of a gun. The paper carried a long list of 'useful and costly presents' such as furniture, tea and dinner services, silver dishes and linen. The church choir gave a plated butter dish and there were watercolours, perhaps gifts from village artists.

Cecil Arnold.

After a honeymoon in London the couple lived at Brooklyn. Their first

Wildcroft c1923. In the foreground are Mary Ann and Tom Metcalfe. Tom, on the car bumper, has his grandson on his knee. Dolly stands by the duck punt which was kept pulled up by the garden gate.

son was born on July 1, 1922. He was named Cecil Thomas Metcalfe Arnold, but known as Tom.

The Arnold's second son Robert (Bob), was born a year after Tom. In 1925, Jack (John Francis), followed two minutes later by Olive Mary, completed the family.

The children often had meals at Wildcroft and had to be on their best behaviour, especially when guests were around. Tom aspired to be his grandfather's constant companion and followed him everywhere.

The children attended the village school, built in 1875, which stood in Mill Way. It has now been replaced by a modern building. The old, typically Victorian building had little comfort for the scholars. The parish council records show that the playground was almost permanently flooded.

Tom Metcalfe paid for piano lessons for twins Jack and Olive. They were taught by Cyril Asplin who lived in the village and was church organist for many years. One Christmas the twins practised a duet for the school concert. Unfortunately, during the performance once of them played a wrong note causing the other to lose time. A heated squabble ensued and in Jack's words, 'they packed up'. Jack didn't play again but Olive continued.

During the annual Feast Week, a highlight of the year for the children, the road would be closed from Briar Cottage, Holywell, to the Rose and Crown at Needingworth. This allowed for the parking of the caravans and vehicles. Sometimes problems were caused by the noise and inconvenience endured by people living closest to the scene. Suggestions to move the fair to a field were dismissed and appeals were made by the parish council for locals to be more considerate.

The fair was held on the first Sunday after July 18 (St John's Day). Roundabouts, stalls, sideshows and swinging boats created a fantasy world for a few days. There was a fancy dress competition, and a cricket match, and the St Ives Town Band played to entertain the villagers from the surrounding area.

Another annual event was

Tom, Bob and the twins on the wall at Wildcroft. Dolly and Tom Metcalfe stand behind, with a guest by the gate. On the back of this photograph is written: 'From J.M. Prior, September 1928. What we saw on the wall at happy Holywell. Where's the missus?'

This school photograph dates from the late 1920s. Not all the children's first names are known, but from left to right, back row, they are: Bob Arnold, Tom Arnold, Harry Odell, ? Masterson, J Parr, Vic Odell.
Middle row: ? Few, Mabel Edwards, Evelyn Coulson, R Hemington, G Pryor, Dick Childs, ? Few.
Front Row: Dorris Gilson, Betty Payne, Ivy Burling, Joan Coulson, Hazel Seekings, Betty Campling, Hester White.

Plough Monday. This custom was dying out and as far back as 1891. The *Hunts County Guardian* called it an absurdity – 'an excuse for horse-play and a great deal of begging'. However shopkeeper Chris Bedford had his own version of the custom.

Children would run to his shop in Needingworth on the second Monday in January. He would come out and throw free sweets for them to catch. Sometimes, the bags would contain flour or rotten fruit, causing great hilarity when they burst. More fun than pulling a plough from door to door!

May Day, when there was dancing around the Maypole and the May Queen was chosen, together with the Sunday School tea, were other annual events to enjoy. The church and chapel choirs and

Temperance Society all organised day trips to the coast. Hunstanton and Skegness were reached by greatly enjoyed train or coach journeys. Agricultural shows, local markets, and celebrations of events of national importance provided welcome variety to the daily routine.

The White Horse.

Tom Metcalfe was a keen sportsman who enjoyed singing; his activities ensured he had an active social life. The White Horse pub was often the scene of the football and cricket club dinners. The White Cockade Club sometimes met here and Tom Metcalfe was a member of all three.

In 1899, the cricket club's annual meeting was held at the pub. Sanders Spencer of Manor Farm was captain and Tom Metcalfe vice-captain, while brother Walter was a team member.

Tom Metcalfe outside the White Horse.

The White Cockade Club held a meeting there in the same week. A proposal put to the meeting by the chairman stated: 'The meeting strongly protests against the idea of spending public money or receiving subscriptions to assist in perpetuating the memory of the infamous regicide Oliver Cromwell.' Royalist songs were sung by the chairman, Fred and Walter Metcalfe, J Tabbitt and others.

The outburst of feeling was in reaction to plans to erect a statue in St Ives, to the memory of Oliver Cromwell. The Lord Protector had lived and farmed in St Ives and as a boy attended Huntingdon Grammar School.

Pig-keeping was a country custom which helped to feed the family and guests at Wildcroft. Easy animals to feed, pigs could survive on household scraps, bran and milk. Salted and hung as hams, they

Dolly astride a horse pulling a farm cart.

were an important food source.

On March 12, 1910, a guest wrote in the visitors book: 'The mystery of the pig was not solved except that we did not eat it.' Obviously not all animals were successfully reared! He added: 'I had a splendid time and wish it wasn't the end of the season.'

The Front at Holywell, with Mary Wilmer (née Tabbitt), Olive, Dolly and the family pig. Mary had time for everyone and was the village news gatherer. Village children regarded her as their 'aunty' and she was Dolly's great friend.

Other types of home production could fail. In August 1911 another guest noted: 'Have had a ripping time, but it's a pity that the hens and cows ran so dry.'

However, most guests were more than satisfied. In April 1911, a Mr Gray commented: 'It is an entirely mistaken idea to sew buttons on with thread. It should be elastic.' George Layton from Sussex, writing in August 1911, summed up the feelings of many guests. He wrote: 'Utopia . . . my visits will be more than hardy annuals. They will become a habit.'

After a few years, Dolly and Cecil separated and Bob

went to live with his father's family. Bob and Cecil often visited the other children. Tom spent a great deal of time with his grandparents, while Dolly cared for the twins.

Traditionally, women helped on the land and Dolly had always enjoyed rush-cutting. She also worked for local farmers at haymaking and harvest time. Olive and Jack remember running to the fields after school, to be with her.

Before farm mechanisation, plenty of hands were needed to bring in the harvest. If the weather were right, people worked by moonlight to complete the task. In 1945 the *Hunts Post* reported that RAF personnel, local volunteers and 3,000 prisoners of war, helped bring in the crops.

Jack Metcalfe and Geoffrey Pearson help with the harvest after school. The horse drag they are using was driven up and down the field after the main crop was lifted to collect remaining hay.

A 'horkey' or harvest supper was held on the last day of harvest. In September 1898, the *Hunts County Guardian* described such a gathering at Manor Farm, Holywell. Mr Sandifer said how pleased he was to see everyone at their twenty-third celebration. He remarked: 'Happily the harvest had been gathered without any drawback, unpleasantness or accident'. The company enjoyed roast beef, plum pudding, games and dancing.

Farmers also employed boys. They worked at weekends, before and after school. Jack remembers haymaking at Portholme near Huntingdon, for farmer Joe Roberts, of Holywell Manor.

Pictured outside Brooklyn are Jack in his naval uniform, Michael Parkinson, an evacuee from Kilburn (related to the Tabbitts), family friend Reg Hudson and, in front, Bob holding Tinks, and Dolly.

Portholme meadow, thought to be the largest meadow in Europe, lies a short distance from the causeway where Oliver Cromwell is reputed to have fallen into the marsh. He was saved by a clergyman named Johnson who, meeting Cromwell years later, is said to have rued the deed.

Jack and his brother Tom also looked after cattle grazing the verges at Holywell. They would lead the beasts out in the morning and back to the farm in the evening. The grazing was auctioned yearly, usually in the local pub. In March 1900 the *Hunts County Guardian* reported: 'Messrs. King & Son let the herbage of the Parish Banks, Droves & Roads by public auction'. Farmer J Butcher obtained the bank grazing from Overcote to the Ashtree for £8.10s and from the Ashtree to Holywell for £4. The 'Ashtree' mentioned is thought to be the tallest tree, on the right of the front cover painting of this book.

Mary Ann would often send Olive to the village shop to buy peanuts. These together with a glass of ruby port were small treats she enjoyed.

On May 11, 1939, the *Hunts Post* recorded that Mary Ann Metcalfe had died after being confined to bed for three months. She was seventy-one. The oldest man in the village, Fred Tabbitt, died in the same week. He had been employed by pig-breeder Saunders Spencer at Holywell Manor, and had been a church chorister for twenty years.

Mary Ann was spared the experience of seeing her grandsons go to war. Jack was awarded five medals for service aboard the vessels *Lady Kathleen, Ondina, Daldorch, Ranchi* and *Swift*. He never married. Maisie, his wartime sweetheart, was killed by a bomb. In 1947 Jack began work as a driver at RAF Wyton and he received the Imperial Service Medal on retirement in 1987.

Bob joined the RAF and spent time in Kaiphur, India. He was awarded the Defence and Victory

Tom Arnold, an RAF navigator, is pictured third from right in front of a Lancaster bomber.

medal. Bob worked for engineers Baker Perkins, St Ives Sand and Gravel Company and the county surveyor's office. In 1950 he married Margaret Papworth and they had one son, Stuart.

The wartime evacuees billeted in the village were helped to feel at home by the locals. An account in the *Hunts Post* in September 1939 thanked those in Holywell-cum-Needingworth who gave donations for Christmas presents for the evacuees.

The area, dotted with airfields, was the home of the Pathfinder Force. Locals quickly recognised the engine noise of the different aircraft flying on operations.

Tom Arnold had won a place at Huntingdon Grammar School, where his teachers recognised his excellent brain but his peers found him blunt and rustic – steeped as he was in the ways of the countryside. His brilliant mathematic ability destined him to become a sergeant navigator. He served on Avro Lancaster bombers with 138 and 161 Squadrons.

Tom Metcalfe in old age.

Tom had what is euphemistically termed an 'interesting war', gaining three medals. He met Special Operations Executive members Odette and Peter Churchhill, who worked with the French Resistance; a menu bearing their autographs was one of his mementos. Another keepsake is a notebook for navigators. Chillingly, it contains navigational calculations for the bombing of Turin and Arras.

Tom recounted an RAF tale to Joe Newell, author of *The Holywell Story*. While flying along the Ouse valley, Tom's plane passed over Holywell. It roared as they gained height over the church. Beatty Carter, landlady of the White Horse, straining to see it, fell down the pump hole, breaking her ankle and a crate load of beer. On hearing the outcome of his aerial viewing of his home, Tom decided to keep mum.

In October 1945 a village social organised by the British Legion raised £10 towards the troops' homecoming fund. A welcome home reception, together with a street party, was held outside the Queen's Head, Needingworth.

Punt-gunner, wildfowler, rush merchant, fisherman, eel-catcher, hive-maker, punt-builder, convivial host and sportsman, Tom Metcalfe also served as a parish councillor. During those years he was a member of various committees, caretaker of the banks and droves and trustee of a number of village charities. In 1933, he was a member of the committee considering the installation of street lighting. In 1935, there was a request for a 30mph speed limit and in 1937 for the installation of a village telephone box. The main water system was available to all by 1939.

During the last three years of the war Tom Metcalfe's health failed and he became blind. In December 1945 he died aged eighty, after being bedridden for eighteen months. The *Hunts Post* reported: 'As a fisherman and rush cutter, he was known by a large number of people from all over the country, who used to visit Holywell in the fishing season.'

Tom Arnold was granted leave to attend the funeral. In 1946 he was demobilised and took over his grandfather's business.

Mercifully, Dolly's two other sons also returned safely from the war.

After the danger, travel and excitement of the RAF, Tom was happy to settle to a countryman's life once more. Tom Metcalfe's patient training had not been

Tom Arnold with the tools of his trade.

28

At Tom and Alma's wedding reception are, back row, Bob and his wife Margaret, twins Olive and Jack. Seated, are Alma, Tom and Dolly, and Olive's daughter Diana is in front. Olive married Jack Parr in 1948 and had four children, Diana, Michael, Richard and Nigel.

obliterated. Tom Arnold had always had a yearning (but never the opportunity), to become a doctor. Now, he followed this interest by studying medical books. There were people in the village who would take his advice, rather than consult a doctor.

The Ferry Boat Inn changed hands several times after the death of the Jacksons. Although the Metcalfes had no longer any family connections with the inn, its situation ensured a continuing association. In 1955 Tom Arnold met the new barmaid, Alma Dodd. One day on his way along the riverside path, Tom is said to have stuck his head through the bar's open window and said to Alma, 'We're getting married'. The ceremony took place in April 1957 and the reception was held at the inn. Alma and Tom's successful partnership was to last for twenty years. After the wedding, Alma left her job at the inn and she and Tom moved into Wildcroft, which had been let after Tom Metcalfe's death.

This unsigned watercolour of the Inn may have been painted by one of the Frasers' students. It is unusual in that it depicts the scene in the harshness of winter, rather than the soft lushness of summer.

THE FERRY BOAT INN

The thatched inn and barn with drawbridge.

The Ferry Boat Inn used to be two separate dwellings. They were the inn, The Boat, facing the river, and Ferry Cottage facing west. The cottage's gable end is seen on the left in the photograph on the previous page. A row of cottages used to stand behind the inn and one is just visible to the leftin the painting on page 29. The inn was built at what was an important crossroads into the Fens, where road and river meet. It claims to be the oldest in England and certainly there has been an inn on this site for centuries. The Saxon, Hereward the Wake, is said to have crossed at this place, during his campaign against William the Conqueror.

To celebrate Oak Day the ferry is fitted with additional poles forming triangles that are decorated with Chinese lanterns, oak leaves and rushes. Two figures stand on the ferry. Jack Arnold thinks that the man in the boat could be his grandfather. The photograph dates from 1892.

Willows and rushes mark the river's edge and flat water meadows stretch from the river's southern bank. When the mist hangs thickly over the river, mystery clings and distorts the scene.

A white lady, the ghost of Juliet Tewsley, is reported to haunt the inn. She was thought to have been spurned by handsome but callous and hard-drinking woodcutter, Thomas Roul, and to have hanged herself in sight of the building in 1050. Suicides were denied rest in consecrated ground and were buried at crossroads and on county boundaries – a ruse intended to confuse the ghost, should it return. As the inn was extended, Juliet's grave became enclosed in it. Her reputed gravestone can be seen laid as a floor stone. On March 17 the large flat slab is said to move and Juliet may appear.

Tom and the inn's proprietor at the time, Daphne Edwards, once played an elaborate hoax on March 17. Daphne, dressed as Juliet, was punted past the inn by Tom, also disguised. Ian Hogan, (at the appointed time) looked towards the window and pointed to the scene. People rushed to the window to view the apparition; unfortunately, Daphne had a fit of the giggles and everyone recognized her laugh.

The inn owned the right to operate the ferry at Holywell. The wooden drawbridge was moved across the river by winding a continuous chain on a winch. People, vehicles, cattle and sheep could be carried across, saving on journey times. Sheep could be taken half-way across, then the tail board dropped so that they could swim to the other side – cleaning the fleece *en route*.

In 1947, at the height

Left, part of the wrecked drawbridge in front of the Ferry Boat Inn in 1947.

of the floods, Hugh Watson bought the Ferry Boat Inn. The inn often looked out across a sea of water.

Before modern drainage and staunches were in place, the river was tidal to Holywell. The water rose to the height of the inn's terrace wall, where boats could be moored. Ian Hogan, barman for twenty-one years, remembered the area often being flooded from Christmas to Easter.

The catastrophic flooding of 1947 caused widespread devastation throughout the Fenlands. Unprecedented winter snowfalls and freezing conditions preceded a sudden rapid thaw. A hurricane blew on the evening of March 16, exacerbating the problems. The river banks at Over were breached, allowing the waters

Drawbridge of the type lost in 1947.

free rein. They entered the inn, flooding the old kitchen, scullery and cellar.

The Pike and Eel – once owned by Oliver Cromwell's cousin, General Hampton, and which also operated a ferry to the Cambridgeshire bank – was so badly flooded that it was evacuated and the drawbridge sank. With the help of the military, the breach at Over was closed. Amphibious vehicles carrying gault clay and using submarine netting stemmed the flow of water. Then huge pumps were used to speed the water away.

In the 1930s the Holywell ferry had been

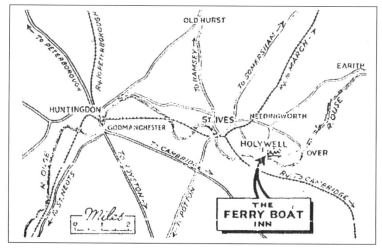

replaced by a smaller version, made by carpenter W Senescall. It was hand-pulled my means of a cable but, by 1946, infrequent use resulted in it being taken out of service. The ferocious gale which blew in March 1947, during the flood, lifted the ferry over the willows into the meadow. Wally Tabbitt was one of the gang of men who tried to rescue it. It was a Herculean task under the prevailing conditions, not helped by the proprietor's wife plying them with rum. In the end, the raging current broke it up and carried it off.

The ceiling of the bar was covered with the autographs of servicemen, for the inn was a popular place for off-duty relaxation. A song entitled *Down at the Ferry Boat Inn* was thought by locals to have been written about it. Played by the bands of the time, it was recorded on a Decca 78 record by Benny Lee in 1950. One of the eel hives made by Tom Arnold hung over the fireplace in this bar. American servicemen liked to take these back home as souvenirs. Tom told them they were exhaust pipes for horse-drawn vehicles!

Tom Arnold at the bar of his 'office'. On the wall behind him is an eel hive.

A raconteur and wit, Tom was also a fount of knowledge. He acquired a full set of *Encyclopaedia Britannica* and regularly added to his already considerable knowledge. In his back pocket he kept a notebook full of his collected snippets of information. Quiz teams vied to claim him as a member.

Visitors, fishermen and people boating on the river all recognized the tall, well-built figure, who lived on The Front at Holywell. He symbolized the village and the independent country life which others envied.

Above, left, marooned by flood water in 1959.

Reminiscent of the watermen of bygone years, Tom had a tally for drinks which accumulated for him at the inn. The old lightermen's beer allowances (part of their wages) was chalked up on boards outside the inns – crossed off when it was consumed. Tom's tally consisted of cocktail sticks stuck into a methuselah cork – a 'wand' removed when a pint was drunk.

Like his grandfather before him, Tom enjoyed singing. Folk songs were his favourite and at one time he held The Saturday Club at the Inn. Friends who liked to sing would congregate on Saturday mornings wearing their club ties – blue, with an angel and halo embroidered motif.

Tom revelled in being the centre of attention and wasn't above a little jocular arrogance. Once, when asked if he had completed the *Telegraph* crossword, he replied: 'Did it while I stirred me coffee!'

PUNT-GUNNING

om Metcalfe was a professional punt-gunner working on the Great Ouse, downstream from Wildcroft. Ducker's Hole was one of his favourite places – named after an unfortunate man who drowned there. He often spent uncomfortable hours lying prostrate in the gun-punt in the cold dawn light, peering through mist and thoroughly doused in its moisture.

Before the drainage of the fenland, the meres and winter floodlands teemed with birds and fowl of everydescription. Tens of thousands of migrants arrived from October onwards, a vast food resource for the inhabitants and a valuable commodity to send to market.

Thomas Metcalfe in a gun punt in front of Wildcroft.

In the days before the protection and conservation of birds, any could grace the countryman's plate. People ate duck, goose, widgeon, quail, pheasant, grouse, pigeon, lark, rook, swan, sea birds, heron, bittern, corncrake and plover. Even starlings and sparrows were baked in pies.

punt gun

A flock of swimming or wading birds required a special gun for maximum effect. The punt gun, which was operated from a gun punt, served the purpose. A monster of destruction, the gun enabled one man (or two working together) to harvest a bumper bag of birds. Officially, there would be five months punt-gunning a year. Shooting was prohibited from March to the August 1. However, independent fenmen were never keen to observe such things to the letter.

In 1901 the *Hunts County News* reported prices of birds from the poulterer as: widgeon 6d, geese 1/6d, plover 2fid, peewits 4d, mallard 9d-1/6d, snipe 6-9d. A price list for the 1999-2000 season gives the following prices: mallard £3.50, teal £1.85, snipe £1.85, woodcock £4, hare £5, pigeon £1, partridge £2, pheasant £2.50, grouse £4.

Punt-gunners made around £1-2 a week, good money at the time – but they could go for up to three weeks without a shot.

Gentleman took up punt-gunning as a pastime. A *Hunts County News* report told of amateurs causing chaos. A professional gunner recalled that he had seen an 'amatoor' craft when he was about four hundred yards from a flock of birds. The 'amatoors' lay with their heads down and their breeches up and were splashing the water. The geese lifted their necks and the 'amatoors' fired, killing one goose. They tried eight more shots and bagged next to nothing. 'We shan't be able to get near no birds again this year. Let's out the bottom o'their blooming punt!' he exclaimed.

Punt-gunning was Tom Metcalfe's most dangerous pursuit.

Mallard duck and drake

His gun was about nine feet long with a rounded stock that allowed the recoil to be taken on the shoulder. Gunners guarded their territory jealously. They were not above firing warning shots to scare sporting strangers from their precious birds.

These fearsome weapons could be turned to other targets. In the early nineteenth century, when wheat prices soared and agricultural wages dropped, fenmen found themselves in a desperate position. Starving thieves were punished by hanging and a group of men in Littleport decided to take action. During the ensuing riots, whatever tools could be found were used as weapons. Their finest weapon consisted of a cart on which were mounted four punt guns – a terrifying sight! However, most of the rioters were hanged or deported.

The gun punts had flat bottoms and

Right above: Tom Metcalfe with his nine-foot punt gun.
Right below: Tom Metcalfe paddles his punt down river.

Tom Metcalfe primes his gun.

could be used in the shallow water of flooded fields. They were curved at both ends. There was no decking but wooden supports took the gun, allowing just enough space for a man to sit behind it. The punt could be shoved (punted by a long pole), or quietly paddled by means of two short handed rounded paddles – like table tennis bats. Light in the water, they could also be sailed. Most gunners made their own punts from whatever wood they could find. Tarred and waterproof they would last for years.

Many gunners left their guns loaded ready for use, but this was a risky practice which often resulted in misfires and horrible accidents. Cleaning the barrel was the first priority. Then, coarse powder was trickled down the barrel from a rough measure kept in a sawn off bullock's horn. Next, two

Widgeon

sheets of newspaper were rammed down the barrel, followed by about a pound and a half of shot – equivalent to today's No 4 shot. The gun was given a firm shake and placed flat on the punt; a feather was used to apply the priming powder and the lid of the firing cap was dropped.

Keeping the various items dry in the circumstances was an art in itself. Much of the skill of the punt-gunner lay in his knowledge of the habitat and habits of the birds. Finding and approaching the flocks without being seen was crucial to success. Often, birds would be scared by noises out of the control of the gunner, many hours of patient stalking ending with an empty bag.

Moorhen

41

Checking the rear before firing was essential as the recoil pushes the boat backwards for about twenty yards. The gunner would sight along the top of the barrel, cock the hammer and pull the trigger, remembering to turn his head to avoid the trail of black smoke. Jack Arnold recalls a friend who went blind as a result of omitting this last vital movement.

As the noise of the firing was deafening, there was no opportunity for

Tom Arnold stands like his grandfather before him, with a small punt gun, 'tittler', resting on his shoulder.

a second shot. Retired puntgunner, Ernie James, who is in his nineties, remembers that he often had his eyebrows singed or he toppled out of the punt into the icy water, when he was punt-gunning. Ernie said: 'Morning was best for punt-gunning, as it was easier to collect any wounded birds as it got light.' He would go out before dawn and lie in the punt facing east; his biggest bag with one shot was forty-eight birds. Jack Arnold says that his grandfather was always modest about the number of birds he shot but he did reveal that his largest bag stood at fifty-three duck at one firing.

Widgeon were plentiful and their habit of keeping tightly together aided the gunner. A shoulder gun would often be carried in the punt to kill any wounded birds.

When the flood waters turned to ice, the gunners took their guns out on sledges to reach the flocks.

Innkeepers kept a look out for returning gunners. They would prepare a mixture of warmed beer, sugar and ginger to revive them. Fenmen have a reputation for story-telling and many tall tales have

Tom Metcalfe lies flat in his punt, maintaining a low profile as he silently moves his craft to within firing range of a flock of wildfowl.

been told about the number of birds taken by one shot. Congregating in local hostelries to thaw their frozen, aching limbs, gunners would warm to their stories and exaggerate exploits beyond belief. Garrulous quarrels often ensued, degenerating into alcohol-fuelled fisticuffs.

Tom Metcalfe's gun was sold to Peter Standen, an amateur gunner, whose family owned FA Standen, the world-famous agricultural machinery manufacturer and engineering business. Peter and Tom Arnold were friends and Peter often brought his boat to Holywell. He was also an amateur artist with a great interest in birds. Ernie James remembers that Peter used to go punt-gunning on the Ouse Washes with Will Kent, a professional gunner. When Peter retired from gunning, the punt gun was displayed in the Ely Maltings for several years.

The more efficient draining of the fens resulted in a reduction in the sustainable number of birds. After the Second World War there was a huge decline in the number visiting the area. Peter Scott,

The gunner sights along the top of the barrel, cocks the hammer and pulls the trigger, remembering to turn his head to avoid the trail of black smoke.

Peter Standen outside the Ferry Boat Inn during the freezing weather of 1963, when more than a hundred swans congregated to be fed.

who became a wildfowler on the Ouse washes when an undergraduate at Cambridge, became a champion and protector of wildfowl.

In 1954 the Protection of Birds Act gave protection to all birds except pigeons and crows. This dramatically reduced the number of birds which could be shot. Game birds could be shot under licence with a certificated gun and permission from the landowner.

The Wildfowl Trust, with Peter Scott at its head, was established in 1968. One of the last professional punt-gunners, Josh Scott, became warden of Welney Wildfowl Refuge.

In 1981 there was a new Act to protect all birds with the exception of those that damaged crops or public health.

Punt-gunning had become a sport rather than a profession. Only the smaller guns were allowed to be used. Tom Arnold bought a 1.25 inch bore gun from Will Kent. The gun was named 'Tittler' (Tiddler), as it was the custom for gunners to name their weapons.

The 'Tittler'

PUNTS

The regularly rising waters of the tidal Great Ouse often lapped at Wildcroft's garden gate. Tom Metcalfe built punts for his work on the river and for transport. Made of wood, the punts measured sixteen feet by four feet and they had identical rounded, deck-covered stems (ends), allowing them to be 'shoved' from either end. Flat-bottomed, the punts sat low in the water, an advantage when the fen winds blew. They were covered with tar which Tom extracted from old batteries – a hazardous task often resulting in an explosion. The weighted punts were sunk in the river until the wood was swollen and the joints tightened.

Local fishermen and the

This photograph of the river and Ferry Boat Inn has, in the foreground, a punt of the type used to transport people and rushes. The man in the craft has not been identified, but he bears a strong resemblance to Tom Metcalfe.

Tom Arnold was fearless on the river and would cross when it was in full flood. Here he is seen paddling a punt during the 1947 flood. The waters have subsided from their peak and Tinks the dog enjoys the trip.

sportsmen who stayed at Wildcroft used the punts.

People living by rivers learned to use small craft as a form of transport, although not many learned to swim. It was common for riverside villages to hold regattas in the summer months.

In August 1898 it was reported in the *Hunts County News*, that Mr MHF Fuller had sailed from St Ives to Lowestoft, with C Vincent as his cabin boy. He had entertained the White Cockade Club to a smoking concert aboard his yacht, *Wild Duck*, before he set sail in the last week of July. Described as 'a thorough sportsman', Fuller was also a successful organiser. He presidedover the regatta meeting at Holywell in June 1899, before his trip to Lowestoft.

The regatta was to be held in July, which turned out to be a remarkable month for summer weather. The newspaper reported a mean temperature of 85 F for any given twenty-four hours, 21 above average. The wheat harvest in Cambridgeshire was to start at the end of July.

The regatta held a varied programme of events – sailing, punt, sculling and oars races, swimming races and walking the pole. The punt race was dominated by one family, the Metcalfes. The first heat was won by Walter Metcalfe, the second by Fred Metcalfe, the third by Thomas Arthur Metcalfe and the fourth by A Harper. In the final, Walter Metcalfe came first, Thomas Metcalfe second.

The water polo was won by the St Ivans' team 2-0 and the sailing race was abandoned due to a fading breeze. The day ended with a promenade concert held in the vicarage grounds. The St Ives Band provided the music.

An incident which happened at the regatta was reported under the heading: 'A Boat Sinks. Ladies get a Ducking'. A boat ferrying women across the river began to sink. Despite their cries for help, nobody moved. Eventually, the women found they were able to stand and walked to the bank, rather shocked, and they changed their clothes at a nearby house. The mishap on the river was 'kodaked' – a novelty at the time.

At the beginning of August the postponed events were held and land races included. These were smoking, egg and spoon, throwing the cricket bat and kicking the football races. Mr Fuller's *Gnat* won the sailing match. Strangely, a reprise of the previous calamity took place. A Mr Fuller, perhaps the organiser himself, borrowed a punt to take a 'lady' across the river. She was carrying a red sunshade and wearing large boots. In midstream, the punt gave a lurch, tipping the passenger into the water. A crowd gathered at the scene and Mr Scard ran to the ferry and dived into the water. Under the bobbing straw hat and sunshade he found a youth! Apparently, Mr Scard took it all in good part, saying, 'If he had been tried, he had not been wanting'.

This was the first regatta of its type to be held in Holywell, and with a shorter programme it became an annual event.

As well as organising the regatta, Mr Fuller founded the village football club. In 1889 the football dinner was held at the Ferry Boat Inn. Walter and Tom Metcalfe were present and sang while accompanied by Mr Scard on the banjo and his daughter on the piano.

A picnic party on the Fen Drayton bank, opposite Wildcroft.

In October 1889 derogatory letters about the team appeared in the *Hunts County News*. They were described as 'boys better suited to playing with feeding bottles and trumpets'.

At the annual dinner, babies bottles hung on a plant on the table with trumpets hanging above. The chairman commented: 'It was better to start playing as boys, as it would extend their knowledge'. So, they had the last laugh. By November 1899 the club had one hundred members. The boys' club was inaugurated for very young boys and schoolboys. A new ball was bought and the boys had 'a good go at it', followed by a tea.

Sid Tabbitt remembers that Tom Metcalfe used to charge local boys a penny (1d) to use a punt. Sometimes, boys would simply 'borrow' a craft. If Mary Ann saw a punt go by she would call to Tom Metcalfe – 'them Tabbitt boys have pinched a boat again'. Sometimes his reply would be, 'Go pick caterpillars off the cabbages. They'm paid'.

The punts were used to ferry people across the river – especially after the drawbridge was washed away. Olive vividly remembers taking a group of fishermen across one day. For some reason, her grandfather told her to keep all the men at one end of the punt. Halfway across the river the punt began to go down in the middle, its contents spilling into the water. Unable to swim, Olive managed to grab hold of the floating pole and a fisherman pulled her to the bank. Luckily, no one was injured but the baskets and fishing gear remained at the bottom of the Ouse.

Tom Metcalfe passed on his punt-making skills to his grandson, who developed and improved the design. Tom Arnold built his punts in the barn in the orchard. He used keruing, a timber from south-east Asia, for the framework of the punts – the wood has a 20% bending strength and is 40% stiffer than oak. The front of the punt was slightly pointed but the decks were the same width at each end. Knot-free parana pine was used for the sides, transoms and decks. Tom discovered the benefit of substituting rot-proof, galvanised sheet metal for wooden bottoms.

Tom Arnold in his boat shed.

Sealant was applied between the wood and metal, with pitch and red lead painted on the metal. All wooden parts were painted with Oakham, black or green bitumous paint. Like his grandfather,

Tom sunk the punts in the river before use, to tighten the joints.

Tom bought 16ft poles for his punts. Varnished, they were modified with the addition of a pole shoe of his own design – an old hay fork, the two tines shortened, before it was attached to the pole.

Usually, maintenance of punts was carried out in the spring, as and when the weather and sporting seasons allowed. Alma was always keen to help and in latter years, Tom Arnold employed young men to help with the work. At one time he had a fleet of fourteen punts for hire. Alma helped,

These punts caught in the frozen snow and ice of winter present a chilling scene, in sharp contrast to the idyll of punting in warm, drowsy summer days.

The Front at Holywell looking west during the 1959 flood. A tractor rescues a car from the water. Tom's punts are seen moored outside the fishing barn.

The view eastwards during the 1959 flood. Tom and a friend lean on the garden gate. A punt is moored by the gate and punt poles are propped by the fishermen's barn where the rest of the craft are moored. The Ferry Boat Inn sign stands in water and a cruiser moored by the willows indicates where the river bank lies.

charging £1 a day for a punt. The business petered out in the 1970s when stringent regulations governing the hire of boats were introduced. Tom was quite happy for people to borrow the punts instead.

The craft were used in the village punt regatta, which was revived and ran for five or six years in the 1970s; airmen stationed nearby joined in the fun. The regatta course ran from Morton's field to the Ferry Boat Inn – against the current. Jack Arnold, Peter Buckland, John Napper and Danny Morgan formed a team calling themselves The Plodders. Jack remembers shoving the punt's stern first, made them travel faster; they proved to be a champions!

In June 1913, Mr and Mrs Bertram Crosse from Kent wrote an entry in the visitor's book at Wildcroft – ' . . . have so much enjoyed the sculling and we are looking forward to coming back and renewing our friendship with Holywell. Shall often be thinking of Mrs. M... my only regret is that I didn't have a punting lesson from Mr. Metcalfe.'

During the winter Tom Arnold kept a log fire burning in the grate at Wildcroft. As he sat, drink in hand, the scent of woodsmoke would evoke yarns and reminiscences to be exchanged with friends.

Alma wades out to a man in a punt,
probably during the 1959 floods.

Punts having their yearly maintenance work of scraping, repairing, and painting, on the green outside Wildcroft.

FISHING

When lying half awake
On a bed of feathers drowsy,
And casement window to the world is thrust
The smell of mint and osier,
Marsh peppermint and clover
Come misty flowing dreamy
From the river, the river without doubt.
The sounds of early morning,
The heron's harsh note calling,
The birds that cry among the reeds.
The silent river swirling,
Slipping by and pushing
Past the shallows, where the pike so often feeds.
(Next verse next time.)

Water mint

54

This incomplete poem was penned by a guest from Cheltenham, who stayed at Wildcroft in 1918. His name is illegible and the promised last verse does not feature anywhere in the book. The verse records the vegetation and bird life, while evoking a sensuous picture of the river at the time.

People used to be happy to include coarse fish in their diet and inland fishermen (and women), supplied the fish. After the First World War, tastes changed; coarse fishing became a sport.

Men such as Tom Metcalfe turned their skills to serving the gentlemen anglers. They provided bait, found swims and transported the men to them – sometimes feeding the swims in readiness for the men to cast their first lines.

The Great Ouse was renowned for its excellent fishing. Holywell drew day fishermen and those wishing to stay for longer. Comments in Wildcroft's visitor's book such as: 'Came for a week and stayed on five week's more!' are common.

Tom Metcalfe was well placed to earn a living in this way. One guest commented: 'What Mr. Metcalfe does not know about this river, no one does.' There are many references to the fish caught; bream, roach, perch and pike. In 1909, a guest recorded: 'Catch of the season, three rudd weighing 6lbs.' In 1913 a German visitor recorded his catch as fourteen fish, almost certainly pike – 'two on 1.5lb, three on 2.5lb, five on 4lb, two on 5lb, one on 8lb, one on 8.5lb'. The sketch below was drawn in the visitors' book next to signatures in what looks like identical writing. They are HP Harper from Cape Colony and FE Wiles of Putney. Tom smiles happily as he watches a fisherman.

Tom Metcalfe fishing..

In August 1909 a Mr Scott and his son Cyril, from Cambridge, left a sketch of barely filled scales and this comment on leaving Wildcroft. 'A complete holiday for ourselves (and for the fish).'

Despite Tom Metcalfe's expert advice, fishermen were not always successful. One fisherman left the words: 'Tom showed me all the favourite spots of the fish so favourite that the fish would not leave them'.

Other messages were slightly more encouraging: 'Weather too unsettled for much sport but fish bite well at Ducker's'.

September 1913 saw fifteen 'cycling barmen' visit Wildcroft. They left the following rhyme in the book.

Fifteen visitors, mostly male.
Little water and that is stale.
The fish apparently all away.
All hope to meet another day.

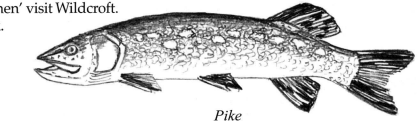

Pike

An exasperated EH Parker of Cambridge left the following:
'Every attention shown me. Except by the fish.'

56

The advent of bus transport gave ordinary working people the chance to enjoy a day trip to the country. Fishing clubs hired buses to take their members to desirable fishing spots.

Weekend buses arrived at Holywell early in the morning, loaded with eager fishermen. Tom Metcalfe provided for their fishing needs, while Mary Ann produced cakes and afternoon tea, when they came back from the river. Dolly and Olive helped with the teas and with ferrying people across the river.

Fisherman came from Nuneaton, Coventry, Birmingham and the north of England. Harold Green ran coaches from London, which brought people from within a seventy-mile radius of the capital.

When Tom Arnold took over from his grandfather he held the fishing rights on both sides of the river at Holywell – from the Pike and Eel Inn to the railway bridge near St Ives. The angling clubs held competitions on this stretch of river.

Peter Buckland from Ilford, Essex, used to travel to Holywell by

Fishermen's buses parked on the Front at Holywell c1935.

Another angler, another pike – in glorious close-up.

coach in the 1960s. The fare of £6 or £7 made an affordable Sunday treat for fishermen and their families. Peter became a champion angler, winning many trophies. Coach parties continued to come to Holywell until the 1970s.

Many happy hours could be spent fishing, whether the fish were biting or not. Staying at Wildcroft seemed to make people wax lyrical. The following verse was written in the visitors' book by IK Bowling, after a two week stay at Wildcroft with his son. They came from Brentwood in Middlesex.

Tom Bowling he thought he had come down from 'Aloft'
for some fish and a good crib aboard.
So he chose a nice spot – Tom Metcalfe's 'Wildcroft'
Holywell, near St. Ives Huntingford.
Tom M. and his good wife look after you well
good feeding, good birds and good sport and St. Peter will say –
'Here's fish - hip Hooray' when poor Tom again goes 'Aloft
Tom B's son who is with him – 'Chuck it Dad - call it sport!
Why the biggest was only 2lb. that you caught.'

When Tom Arnold and Alma married, she took over much of the work at Wildcroft. She looked after the guests, hired out punts and sold maggots, worms and live bait to anglers, from the fisherman's barn. Early morning tea was also served there. Tom Arnold grew maggots on rotting rubbish and sold them in old tobacco tins (he was a pipe-smoker). He also had a worming patch in the garden, to which was added the plate scraps and tea leaves. It was kept well-watered to produce a good

Chubb

supply of worms. On Saturday mornings the worms were dug ready for the anglers. Live bait (small fish, often perch) was kept in a large metal trunk with holes drilled in it. Water could enter to keep the fish alive, as it was moored to the river bank. Live bait was used by the anglers to catch large fish such as pike. Tiddlers caught could be handed over to Tom for the live bait box.

Perch

Chas Squires wrote in the visitors' book in July 1922: 'We hope to return when the big bream are on the feed.'

Parts of the Great Ouse are famous for the number and size of the bream catches. This has been the case for centuries. A report in the *Peterborough Advertiser* in May, 1936, told of an event said to have taken place in 1895.

'To anglers the word Ouse always conjures the vision of hundreds and hundreds of bream. During July and August 1895, five anglers who visited a certain swim near St. Ives twice a week for five weeks, hooked and returned four tons of bream not including the last night's catch. This they sent by cart to St. Ives in a lorry, piled it in a yard and sent the town crier round to invite those who would, to help themselves to the fish. Even then, there was enough left over to give the local cats the grandest time of their nine lives.'

It was not unusual for 100 bream per person to be caught during fishing matches at Holywell.

Places on the Great Ouse are renowned for pike

Guy Wadsworth and Peter Buckland fish from a punt.

fishing, the pike being in season in autumn and winter months. Pike are the largest fish in the river apart from the rare sturgeon, which are no longer found.

In October 1909 Stuart Pethick, from Liverpool, entered in the visitors' book, a rewrite of a verse of a music hall song.

I've known the Metcalfes for twenty years.
Better hosts I should never wish to choose.
And for Pike, there's no river running in the land,
As I'd swop for the good old Ouse.

When Mary Ann was alive she would cook the fish in the traditional way. It would be stuffed with forcemeat and the tail skewered into the mouth. Brushed with egg and breadcrumbs and basted with butter, it was baked in a hot oven. A spectacular dish to bring to the table, for a guest who had caught the fish.

At the beginning of the twentieth century, eels were regarded as a delicacy. Often fishermen would catch them when angling for other fish. In July 1909 Arthur Clements of Cambridge wrote in the visitors' book after a three-day visit to Wildcroft: 'Eels between 8pm and 6am are the chief speciality this unsettled weather. You catch the eels, Mrs. M will make the parsley sauce! I would I could stay for three months.'

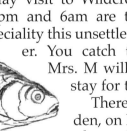

Dr Webb, a frequent visitor who cruised down from Ely in his day boat, holds a fine specimen of pike.

There was a large pond behind Wildcroft's garden, on land belonging to the inn. It was once a pit, where clay was dug for brick- making in the kiln

Roach

near the inn. In modern times the pond was filled in to make the car park. When the river was in flood Tom Metcalfe fished the pond.

Danny Morgan and John Napper were two of the boys who worked for Tom Arnold. Employed from about the age of eleven, they would dig worms, feed chickens, chop logs, punt anglers across the river, cut rushes, maintain and repair punts, all for a few shillings a week. However, they also got expert advice on fishing and, later, shooting, as well as the benefit of the vast amount of knowledge Tom had accumulated during his lifetime. They, and other village boys who worked for Tom, were kept gainfully and enjoyably employed during school holidays. He even supervised them on their first visits to the inn.

John Napper worked part-time for Tom for about twenty years and Danny for about eleven years. Danny was earning about £14 a week when he left in 1975.

Bream

Tom Arnold outside the fishermen's barn displaying what looks like a roach.

GUESTS AND GUNS

Visitors came to Holywell for the shooting, eager to avail themselves of the expertise at Wildcroft. 'Grandfather was the outside man and grandmother worked with the guests,' Jack Arnold explains.

Wildcroft's visitors' book gives a unique picture of guests and their pastimes. It also gives insights into the characters of Tom, Mary Ann and Dolly.

The first entry in the surviving visitors' book was made in 1908. However, many guests remark on having visited on several occasions. German, French, South African and South American guests are recorded as well as British. Aliens filled in a more detailed registration form and some remain in the book.

The first entry reads: 'Delightful fishing, charming scenery, a most hospitable hostess, very comfortable, cooking perfect. Hope to come again soon.'

Later in the same month was penned:

A winter scene from c1900. A sportsman with an old muzzle loader gun stands outside the inn; the water has risen to the bottom of the steps. a duck hangs from a tree.

Dolly, second left, Tom and Mary (when she was aged about fifty), with an unidentified guest.

'Floating down the river chance brought us here, we hope to again put to so comfortable and kindly haven'.

In June 1909 the Reverend JF Tanfield, Rector of Holywell, wrote on behalf of himself and his wife Dorothy: 'Before taking up our residence at the Rectory during our removal and whilst the workman were in possession – I spent many days at Mrs Metcalfes' whose uniform kindness, good cooking and scrupulous cleanliness proved in themselves to be a very hearty welcome to Holywell'. An impeccable reference for Mary Ann!

Jack Arnold says: 'We used to live mainly on wildfowl and game and the guests did as well'. Olive adds: 'Moorhen suet pudding; that was a

Red grouse

marvellous meal'.

Visitors' comments on the food include: 'If Tom could make the pike feed like Mrs Tom makes her guests feed there would soon be none left'; 'the apple charlotte was simply grand'; 'Don't forget to ask for treacle pudding'; 'the stewed eels, oh my'.

Mary Ann was devoted to providing the best for visitors. Jack Harrison remembered that she once walked to the Pike and Eel Inn to borrow a little seasoning (perhaps sage) from his Aunt Nelly. She had run out and wouldn't disappoint her company.

Tom Metcalfe leans on the car radiator and Dolly sits on the running board, a gun across her knees in this 1920 photograph taken outside the Queen's Head, Needingworth. Other members of the shoot lean nonchalently on the car.

Mrs Tom, as guests often referred to her, was by no means subservient. She had a sharp tongue and could nag and hector her guests. In 1914 FB Imbert-Terry from Devon recorded: 'Wish I had brought the wife as I have not been so hen-pecked in my life'. FL Englemen remarked: 'Not even the active tongue of Mrs. M herself could adequately describe the good time we had'.

BR Lummer of 3rd Dragoon Guards (PoW) Punjab India wrote: 'Six years since I was last here and Mrs. M and her tongue still young – I wish she would use it to charm the fish out of the river'.

Dolly helped her mother and entertained the guests. 'Mrs. M and Dolly as kind as usual,' was written by Mr and Mrs Blanch in 1913. While in 1914, HH Gilbert, from Earl's Court, declared: 'A charming daughter but Mrs. M a sharp tongue'.

The previous year, FRH Carew from London left this cryptic message: 'Hope to return in 1916 by which time I trust Dolly will have relented'. Could this mean a rejected proposal of marriage?

Left, Tom Metcalfe and his friend Graham Stanham from Blackheath.

'The night of my life!' was the simple statement left by GN Jenkins in January 1911.

As well as accompanying guests on the shoots, Dolly would sing and play the piano for guests in the evening. In 1911 H Alger of Cambridge left the following note: 'Many thanks to Dolly for the very fine music in the evenings'. There are many such comments. In 1915, I Struell from Croydon wrote: 'Have much enjoyed my stay, particularly the fluent conversation of Mrs. M and the charming music from Dolly.'

Curlew

Poor weather and Mary Ann's indisposition could not mar the visitors' enjoyment. Mr and Mrs Walters noted in 1923: 'Wishes for Mrs Metcalfe's speedy recovery. Dolly filled the breach like the little trouper she is. An enjoyable holiday, that not even the rain could mar.'

Tom Metcalfe was, on the whole, a quiet man but good company when in his element, out shooting. Those who knew him describe him as having a dry wit but he was reserved and suspicious of strsangers – said to be the characteristics of fenmen. However, he was popular with his guests.

Jack Harrison recalled that his uncle and aunt Sydney and Nelly Broughton, bought the Pike and Eel from Mrs Hemmington in 1915. Sydney was a retired wine and spirit merchant from London. He brought three barrels of whisky with him and, as it was war time, the locals soon flocked to the inn. Hearing about the whisky, Tom Metcalfe

Left, Tom Metcalfe and guests. The vehicle behind them could be an early soft-topped Austin. The date is c1937. Right, Jack carries a bag for two gentlemen. They used mainly Churchill and Purdy guns.

arrived too late and was offered ginger beer. 'I'd rather have wild cats running around inside me. We shall never win the war,' he said, and promptly left.

Often large groups of undergraduates would camp in the orchard. They came from Cambridge seeking Tom's instruction and guidance on fishing and shooting. In December, 1908, a group of three from Trinity and Caius colleges recorded these words: 'Sometimes we shoot game and catch fish, sometimes not, but whether we do or not we are capitally looked after, and enjoy ourselves'.

TH Farmiloe of Hampstead wrote: 'A splendid weekend for overworked undergraduates'.

Tom Metcalfe's observation and knowledge of the countryside is reflected in *The Victoria County History of Huntingdonshire* Volume 1, published in 1926. It contains numerous sightings of birds attributed to him. Common at the time were geese, duck, moorhen, heron, coot, corn-crake, water-rail, redshank, snipe and plover near the Ouse. Others such as curlew, goosander, oyster catcher and tern were rare.

G Graham Stanham was a frequent visitor to Holywell, and in September 1909 he wrote: 'Have visited on and off for nine years, and have always found everything A1'.

The gypsies also considered themselves Tom Metcalfe's friends. They would bring their caravans to Ferry Road on the Fen Drayton Bank and call to him across the river. Tom Metcalfe would punt across and spend an evening with them, usually sharing a meal. Jack Arnold remembers that they used to refer to his grandfather as Missa Metcap. The 1697-1812 marriage allegations records for

Holywell-cum-Needingworth include, in 1783: 'Thomas Meetcap, bachelor to Sarah Holoway, spinster, both of the parish.' Could Metcalfe be a corruption of Meetcap? Has the gypsy's oral tradition almost preserved the ancient name?

Guests often took Mary Ann and Dolly out for a spin in their cars. Jack remembers his mother, her hair blowing in the wind, asking: 'How fast are we going now?' 'Fifteen miles an hour,' came the answer. At this she screamed with disbelief.

Tom Metcalfe held the local shooting rights and took his guests out after game. Duck, pigeon, rabbit, grouse, pheasant and hare went on to the table; any extra was sold.

Dolly and Olive sitting on the back bumper of a hackney carriage, taking a welcome break from the chores.

66

Wood pigeon

The railway reached St Ives in 1847, allowing surplus game to be quickly transported to the London markets.

In 1911, a remark left in the visitor's book read: 'Holywell is a very nice place especially, the ducks and hares.' Jack and Oliver remember that they often ate jugged hare. The joints of hare were browned, then placed into a jar, with seasonings and gravy. The covered jar was put into a pan of boiling water for about four hours. When it was nearly done, forcemeat balls and port wine were added. Dishes like this caused one visitor to describe Mary Ann as 'truly a Cordon Bleu'.

Tom Arnold at fifteen, with what could be his first bag.

Jack Arnold says it was nothing for his grandfather to shoot seven brace of partridge before breakfast. He would walk the three miles along Holywell bank to Hermitage lock, probably stopping for a warming drink with the publican Jack Gilson at Brownshill Staunch, about two miles from home. Or, with John Day who kept The Anchor on Holywell Front.

On his fifteenth birthday, Jack's grandfather gave him a twelvebore shotgun. He also received three cartridges and was expected to return home with something for the pot.

Jack spent many a long hour wildfowling. He says: 'It gets into your blood. If you look out and the conditions are right, you feel impelled to go'. On a clear moonlight night, a wildfowler can easily spot the birds returning to the washes or pools. If the marksmen aren't careful, the birds will spot them too. Dark clothing, balaclava helmets and blackened faces all help to conceal the men in the undergrowth or boat. The birds see the decoys which have been placed in the water, hear the men's

Snipe

whistles and with luck settle on the water. The wildfowler must wait for the birds to come into range of the guns. Those last waiting moments are agonising – pull the trigger too soon and all is lost. Jack's biggest bag was fourteen duck. On another occasion, he shot seven partridge with a single shot. He once came across a flock of forty teal and with four shots bagged nine birds.

The sport was not without danger. Jack knew a man who had lost four fingers in a shooting accident and another who accidentally blew off his own head, hurriedly reaching for a loaded gun, while in a boat.

Tom Metcalfe bred spaniels and at one time had four. Rapture, Ringlet, Bellman and Bondsman earned their keep by retrieving game brought down by the sportsmen.

68

Tom's favourite delicacy was snipe on toast. 'He'd put the toasting fork through the bread doorstep and through the snipe, holding it near the hot embers of the fire,' says Jack. When the bread was toasted the snipe was cooked.

Snipe were plentiful around the Ouse towards Earith. The birds liked the soft boggy ground. They fly upwind when disturbed, so the gunners approach down wind and the snipe fly over them.

The *Hunts County News* reported in 1860 that one gamekeeper shot snipe all day in the marshy fields before drainage and in Whittlesey Washes they were abundant. Numbers unheard of today.

Dolly Arnold helped her mother for many years and eventually took over the running of the guest house. In the days before the taxi service from St Ives railway station, Dolly would collect visitors in the pony and trap – and in her turn, Olive helped with the work.

When Tom Arnold married Alma Dodd she took over the running of Wildcroft. Guests returned frequently to enjoy

Tern

Holywell and Alma's excellent cooking. She taught Tom to cook, and he helped in the kitchen and served breakfast. After Alma's death, Tom held regular dinner parties for friends. They took turns at cooking and Tom was always keen to experiment with new dishes.

Tom Arnold continued to shoot throughout his life and he taught many others the intricacies of the sport. Peter Buckland first came to Holywell on the fishing coaches from London. Later, he stayed at Wildcroft and finally, he moved to the village.

Tom taught Peter to shoot. He recalls that Tom was very safety conscious; for the first two weeks

Perch Urch, left, and his brother were regular visitors to Wildcroft. He is seen here with Danny Morgan and Tom Arnold's dogs Topo and Maybelle. Behind, rushes are drying over wires and the Ferry Boat Inn with its 1968 extension can be seen.

Peter was allowed only to handle an empty gun. Tom insisted that a shotgun must be broken when carried. After safety the most important lesson was in the ways of wildlife and their habitats. Peter Buckland always shot for the pot. His bags included rabbit, pigeon, partridge, pheasant, wigeon, pintail and mallard.

Local farmers were grateful to Tom for keeping an eye on their cattle, grazing the pastures at Holywell. In return they invited him to shoot on their land.

EELS AND HIVES

One of the Metcalfe brothers, punting a load of eel hives (traps), to set in the river at Holywell.

The marshes, washlands rivers and dykes of the fens provided the perfect environment for eels. Able to live in fresh and salt water, to travel across land like snakes, to feed on almost any carrion, they were probably the most adaptable fish, and were so abundant that they were used as currency. Rents and other dues were fixed in quantities of eel. The church, in particular, used this method. The Ely monks paid tens of thousands of eels in dues each year.

Their importance in the lives of the population credited them with special powers. Wedding rings were made from the skins and eel skin garters were said to protect the wearer from rheumatism.

From early times, eels smoked, roasted, stewed, fried, jellied or baked in pies provided an important, plentiful food source. Eels have elongated bodies and modified fins to give maximum mobility. Resembling snakes, they can reach areas inaccessible to other fish, as they can swim in any direction. A number of methods were employed to catch eels. In shallow water, 'bobbing' was used. A yard of worsted wool, threaded with earthworms and tied into a knotted ball, was dangled into the water. The eels' teeth were caught in the wool as they took the worm. After the wool was gently pulled, the caught eels were shaken and dropped off – only small eels could be caught in this way. Eels have a strong sense of smell and their teeth are blunt and curve inwards, the jaws being immensely strong. Serrated scissors or grippers were used to hold the slippery heads safely.

Glaiving (gleeving), using a glaive (gleeve), became illegal in 1923. This method involved using a long handled spear, with three or four toothed tines, strengthened by a crossbar. The spear was used from a boat and in clear water the fisherman might see eels poking out of the river bed. Tom Metcalfe is said to have been so proficient he could pole his punt with one end of the glaive and catch eels with the other, as he moved along the river. A story, certainly tinged with fenmen's fancy! The pole, about 12ft long, was heavy to wield – eels would twine around the metal tines and could be lifted into the boat.

Baited lines, nets, grigs and hives made from willow, were used to catch the eels. The larger grips were used mainly in salt water. Mill-wheels often included eel traps, providing additional income for the miller and food for his family.

Adult eels live in fresh water and after eight years their eyes enlarge and their bodies become silvery. Known as silvers, they make their way to sea, wriggling across land when necessary. The journey to the breeding grounds in the Sargasso sea, in the Western Atlantic Ocean, is about 5,000 miles The tiny leaf-shaped larvae hatch and drift with the Gulf Stream. Young elvers reach the European coast about three years later. They swarm up river in their thousands. When caught and cooked, the needle-thin elvers, said to be an aphrodisiac, are a great delicacy.

Eel glaive

Freshwater eels probably spend winter buried in river mud. When the weather warms, the eels begin to move. Active mainly at night, particularly during the time of the new moon, they are fished from April to October. They are most active after the other fish have spawned as they often feed on the eggs. An eel's colour varies according to age and habitat. Dyke eels are often black and river eels green or brown.

The Metcalfes used hives to catch eels. They were set at sunset – often a spectacular time in the fens, when the huge skies are streaked with a myriad tones of yellow, orange and red. The trapped eels were collected early next day.

Tom Metcalfe's father transported eels in a horse-drawn water wagon, which once lost a wheel. In the resulting watery chaos, the slippery catch wriggled to the ground and escaped into the nearby stream.

Tom Arnold attends to his eel trunk on the river's edge.

Locals would buy eels from Tom Metcalfe. Jack Arnold remembers the wife of George Gilson, the St Ives railway crossing keeper, used to cycle to Holywell. Jack's grandfather would fill her willow cycle basket with eels and she would ride off with them squirming in front of her. Eel fisherman Ernie James says that eels like to chew on willow; often congregating under willow trees.

As a boy, Sid Tabbitt would watch Tom Metcalfe kill and skin eels. A quick tap of the head, on the stone floor, and a few deft strokes with the knife completed the operation.

Tom Arnold sets his hives, watched by his dog Pincher. The swamp (island) can be seen across the river. In 1969 Tom Arnold and Joyce Billings of the Ferry Boat Inn bought the area to save it from development.

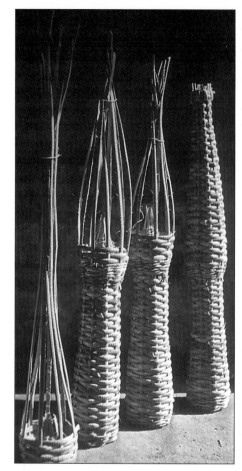

Steps in eel hive making.

The bulk of Tom Metcalfe's catch was sent live by train to Billingsgate and the pie and eel shops of the capital. When she was old enough, Dolly drove the horse and trap the three miles to St Ives railway station. She often raced the trap with its cargo of live eels against the train. If the train reached the level crossing first, the eels missed the London train. However, Dolly detested eels and wouldn't allow them in her house.

It is obvious from the comments in the visitor's book, that Mary Ann cooked a delicious dish of stewed eels with parsley sauce, which came highly recommended.

Eels can live for seventy years and weigh more than ten pounds. When Whittlesey Mere was drained, there were tales of monstrous eels being found. The biggest eel caught by Tom Arnold at Holywell was between five and six pounds.

Tom Metcalfe made his eel hives from willow cut from the swamp or island. The island once belonged to the Manor House and there was a hidden boat

Tom Arnold making his hives

house on it. There were also two ancient fish ponds used for keeping caught fish alive.

Willow was cut in the spring, before the sap began to rise. It is a strong, flexible, natural material, useful for making all kinds of containers. The soaked willow rods were split into three pieces using a small-hand held cleave tool. The split rods woven to make the hive.

The tubular hives were about four feet long and took around four hours to make. Narrow with a wider entrance and two internal compartments, the narrower end held the bait and was closed by a weighted bung.

The eel entered the wider end and smelling the bait, passed through the gate (chair), into the first compartment. The sharpened edges of the gate prevented the eel from returning and it wriggled backwards into the baited compartment. Trapped by the exit bung and unable to pass the sharp edges of the second gate, the eel was caught.

The hives were closely woven using basic basketry techniques. The first gate just inside the entrance can be seen in the hive in the foreground of the photograph on the left. The two central hives show the central gate and the fourth hive is completed.

Tom Metcalfe contentedly smokes his pipe while surveying the river.

Tom Arnold set about refining his grandfather's design. He used split cane instead of willow and found that it lasted four times longer. Tom made hives for other fishermen and, in later years, sold many as decorative items.

He set about twenty hives daily during the season, the traps baited with earthworms. He placed them in areas of the river where he expected eels to be congregating. He left no obvious marker. A twig, a bush or some other natural indicator a discreet distance from the site were his signs. The pole was used to hook the hive out of the water the next day.

Sid Tabbitt remembers that when Tom Metcalfe set his hives, the village boys would often be watching from a hiding place. They would raid the hives early next morning, before Tom went to collect them.

Tom used weighted tobacco tins as bungs for his hives. A hive could contain a number of eels. Tom's biggest catch in one hive was twenty-eight eels. The bung was removed and the eels tipped into the eel trunk. This was filled with holes so that water could enter. It was kept in the river, moored to the bank. When required, the eels were removed live from the trunk. Tom also kept live bait in the trunk for fishing.

Tom sent eels to market and sold them locally. He also jellied eels, which he sold. These were particularly popular with the Londoners who came to Holywell on the fishing coaches. When jellied, eels were cut into lengths and put into the pot with parsley and roughly chopped onion and pepper. Then, covered with vinegar, they were cooked for two or three hours and most of the bones dissolved. Once cool, they could be packed into pots, ready to eat. Always ready to try something new, Tom smoked eels over oak chippings, for his own use. The 1990s saw a renewed culinary interest in the consumption of eel, which had fallen dramatically in recent years. It can now be found cooked in a variety of ways, listed on many restaurant menus.

76

Head of four-prong eel glaive

Swan

RUSH CUTTING

Tom Metcalfe punting home with a load of rushes.

Bulrushes grow in the Great Ouse at Holywell, their chestnut coloured flowers, trembling on tall stems of muted green. *Scirpus lacustris* belongs to the sedge family, in spite of its common name of bulrush.

The Metcalfe family had a flourishing business cutting and selling rushes. The bulrushes' solid stems, which often grow eight feet high with their spiky flowers, were even more abundant at the beginning of the twentieth century. Preferring clean flowing water, they grow at the river's edge or form large beds in bays.

For centuries, rushes were strewn or woven as floor covering. One hundred years ago, rushes were used extensively in making mats, baskets and furniture seats and backs. In those days numerous rush-cutters harvested the rivers, and rush-seaters plied their trade from door-to-door. Another essential use was the caulking of beer barrels and any barrels designed to hold liquids. The Metcalfes had customers in America and Canada and once had an order for rushes for Queen Mary.

Weather conditions permitting, rush cutting began on the first of July. The work was done from a

Left, Tom Metcalfe harvesting rushes at Holywell: Right, his grandson, Tom Arnold.

punt, using a long, slightly curved blade, set at right angles, to a straight, six-foot long handle. The tool is known as a rush knife. The punt is anchored as close to the rushes as possible. Then, the flat knife is pushed down to the river bed and brought up out of the water, under the rushes. They are dragged in and flipped over onto the punt.

It is essential to keep the blade sharp, to enable it to cut cleanly under water. A blunt knife would pull the plants up by the roots.

Until the 1960s, there was about a two yard width of rushes along the banks. About twenty-five yards downstream from the Ferry Boat Inn there was a large bed, known as Morton's bay. There was another bed, near the Pike and Eel Inn, and further ranks along the southern bank. At this time there was only a narrow channel of clear water about the width of a cruiser, down the centre of the river.

The year of 1936 had been the wettest since 1916. In 1937 the ancient elms at Holywell rectory were felled. Having looked down on

Dolly cutting rushes, during the 1950s.

Rush knife

countless generations, their time was over. There was an influenza epidemic which closed the school in Januaryand by the end of the month, St Ives and Holywell-cum-Needingworth were flooded. In the same month a report in the *Hunts Post* stated that the reeds and rushes in the Great Ouse had been removed by a steam dredger, clearing the river channel. 'The rushes were well known and sought after and Mr

Tom Metcalfe was dismayed,' the paper said.

The year continued to be of mixed fortune. In March the village celebrated the coronation of George VI but the event was marred by rain. The troops, on standby because of the floods, eventually stood down on April 1. On Empire Day, April 22, Mrs Harvey lent her wireless for the King's broadcast to be heard, before the village social in the school. The Women's Institute celebrated its twenty-first birthday in June and the year ended amid the heartache and sadness of a diphtheria epidemic.

Dolly tonks an armful of rushes.

Dolly Arnold took over the rush-cutting from her father. Sons Jack and Tom would help, but during the Second World War she had to manage without them.

There is a knack to rush-cutting. The task requires dexterity, strength and a well-developed sense of balance. A smooth slice with the knife ensures that the rushes fall together over the punt. If they miss, it is a dirty, wet job to scoop them out of the river. Rushes are measured in bolts (an armful) and tapping them gets them clean. Next, they are dipped in the river and 'tonked' to clean the butts (bases) of the rushes.

Willow herb

When Dolly started cutting in the 1930s there was

very little river traffic, apart from punts, sailing skiffs, the few remaining lighters (barges) and an occasional Thames punt. Dolly loved rush-cutting and regarded the time spent on the river as a holiday, even though the work is strenuous, involving a lot of bending, lifting and exposure to the elements.

In summer, the water and air around the river are busy with insects. Damsel flies and dragonflies propelled on brilliant, translucent, filigreed wings, dart among the vegetation. The water teems with coarse fish of all types – pike, perch, bream, rudd, eel. The clear, gravel-bottomed water of Morton's bay might reveal a barbel, flounders or smelt. The patterns of swimming snakes and, with luck, playful otters, might be seen. The diamond-strewn, dazzling plumage of a kingfisher, as it leaves the water with a fish, would be the most exotic bird on view. Moorhen, corncake, coot, water rail, swan, heron, grebe, swallow, and the song of warblers would complete the scene.

The river banks are gaudily splashed with purple loosestrife. Reed mace with its chocolate coloured, felty bolsters, clustered in groups, stand by. Yellow flag, tall and sunny and waterlilies, yellow, white and pink, are scattered on the surface of the water. Sweet scented mint and willow herb vie for space along the edge.

Red campion

81

Dolly with a punt load of rushes at Morton's bay. This bay of rushes no longer exists.

The bulrushes no longer achieve the height and thickness of those seen in the photographs on these pages. When cut, they were stacked on the punt, alternately, butts to tips, as can be seen. If the fine weather held, the rush harvest would be over by the end of August. The punt loads of rushes were taken to be dried in a local farmer's field. Dolly spread the rushes in a fan shape on the ground and they were turned once during the drying process. The initial drying could take about two weeks. Care was taken to avoid the rushes drying out too quickly or they became brittle and useless. They need to be kept well aired and protected from damp to stop mould developing. Breweries required thick rushes for caulking but craft workers needed finer rushes.

Dolly working outside the barn tying bolts with raffia ready for sale.

Dolly fans out the rushes to dry.

When the field was no longer available, Tom Arnold devised a method of suspending rushes over wires, erected on the Front. This method grew to be a bone of contention, as people expected free access to the area. Eventually, Tom was forced to give up this method and he dried the rushes on the bank outside Wildcroft instead.

Once cut, the rushes will keep for three to five years, if stored correctly. They are best kept in a dry, darkened barn. The rushes are handled as little as possible, to minimize damage. In dry condition, they are very fragile; once wet they become strong

Tinks and Pincher guard the bolts of rushes ready for dispatch.

*Dolly with a punt load of rushes near Morton's bay. The trees in
the background were lost to Dutch elm disease in the 1970s.*

*Tom is seen in his later years, selling
rushes. He always had a good
rapport with his customers.*

and flexible, and can be woven.

When Tom Arnold returned to Holywell after the Second World War he went to the Ferry Boat Inn for a pint of beer. Discovering that beer was being stored in aluminium barrels, he realized the implications for the rush business. So, he set about finding new markets. Workshops for the blind, Women's Institutes, craft classes, occupational therapists and antique furniture restorers were his customers.

During the 1960s and 1970s Tom had a flotilla of punts leaving the Front during rush-cutting. He employed village boys and students to do the work. Danny Morgan recalls that it took two to three

Rushes suspended over wires for drying at the Front.

hours to cut a punt load of rushes. Tom always instructed cutters to be aware of the wildlife on the river and not to disturb any nesting birds.

Tom Arnold cut rushes up-stream from Browshill Staunch, Earith, to St Ives lock and from Hemingford Abbot's backwater to Houghton. The punts were tied together to pass through the locks. Engines were fitted to some of the punts, which speeded the outward journey and eased the effort of punting home a full load.

Debris from the rushes which collected on the Front sometimes caused problems. Tom's attitude was that when the floods came, the area would be washed clean

Purple loosestrife

naturally, the debris returning to the river.

This reasoning was not always acceptable to the residents.

In the 1960s, Holywell was becoming a desirable place to live. Residents were not necessarily country people, as the old way of living had virtually disappeared.

Tom became a member of the parish council in 1963 and he found himself faced with complaints from villagers who expected him to tidy up. He had no option but to comply.

On average 1,500 bolts of rushes were cut annually. British Rail's three-wheeled trucks used to collect the rushes from Holywell.

Dolly cut rushes until she was in her seventies, although by that time,

Kingfisher

86 Tom would allow her to work for only half a day. An expert, she rarely got wet and never used a motorized punt. Danny Morgan was charged with keeping a friendly eye on her, while she worked.

In recent times there has been more demand for finer rushes as there has been a revival in the use of natural materials. The workmen dredging and maintaining the river need to work closely with the few remaining cutters, to ensure the remaining rush beds are preserved.

Water lily

Great Reedmace

CONCLUSION

Thomas Arthur Metcalfe, countryman and astute businessman, was one of the last independent, successful fenmen to make his living in a variety of ways, according to the season. Jack Harrison, rod merchant and basket-maker, remembered him and described him as 'a very clever man, to get a living the way he did'.

Dolly Arnold spent her young life as an only child, enjoying a more privileged life than the average fenman's child. She grew up at Wildcroft, in contact with the gentry who enjoyed country pursuits. A way of life which declined after the Second World War.

Tom Metcalfe

Dolly spent most of her adult life working hard at Wildcroft, on the land and river, and raising her children. She died in 1971.

Tom Arnold, her son, was known as 'Mr Holywell'. Tom enjoyed a countryman's life of a type that had more or less disappeared elsewhere. He was a local character in every sense. Don Bradley, who lived at Brooklyn after Dolly's death, made a bronze bust of Tom Arnold; this used to stand on the bar in the Ferry Boat Inn. A complex character, Tom was totally happy and content with his way of life, although Alma's death in 1979 left him with a strong sense of loss.

Tom spent hours working out complex mathematical problems supplied by a teacher. His garden gate bore a runic sign. Visitors who

Dolly Arnold

failed to decipher it had to buy Tom a pint. It was, of course, his name!

When people asked Tom what his job was, he would say, 'Don't talk to me about work. I've got my living to earn.'

A member of the parish council for almost thirty years, he bought local knowledge and sound common sense to meetings. After his death, aged seventy-one, in 1994, a development of new houses at Needingworth were named Arnold Close. Tom's brother Bob died a year later.

David Anderson, Tom's farmer friend, devised an annual ceremony to celebrate Tom's memory. At the beginning of July friends gather at the riverside at Holywell, for a blessing of the rushes by the Rector. This is followed by a party with a contest to judge the best brawns – a revival of an ancient custom.

Tom Arnold

The expert on the river has gone. Olive continues to live at Needingworth and Jack in a bungalow built on part of the old orchard. As ever, he keeps a watchful eye on the river's moods and flows. Wildcroft is sold. New houses stand on the site of the orchard and the old boat barn. Only the rush cutting goes on.

The sign on Tom's garden gate.

Felicity Irons, rush-seater and furniture-restorer, used to buy rushes from Tom. After his death, Jack kept the business going for a while but, approaching seventy, he wanted to retire. After a lesson from Jack, Felicity bought a rush knife and a punt and set about cutting. So, a young woman, again cuts the rushes at Holywell. Felicity also designs and makes furniture; she sends table mats to America and also supplies rushes for the floor of the replica Globe Theatre in London.

Sand and gravel have been quarried extensively at Needingworth. In the summer of 1999 plans were put forward to develop a 700 hectare wetland reserve on the site. If this happens the area could again host birds and wildlife long since lost.

Stories of the fens are filled with ghosts. If this area returns again to its watery state, will visitors conjure up the sight of old Tom Metcalfe and his gun punt, drifting out of the morning mist? Will the hazy heat of August shimmer reveal a glimpse of Dolly, bringing in the rushes? Will Tom Arnold's black dogs be heard splashing through the moonlit shallows, to scatter the settling wildfowl? Who knows?

Felicity Irons carries on an old tradition.

Examples of Felicity's work.

BIBLIOGRAPHY

Astbury AK. *The Black Fens*

BBC Radio Cambridgeshire, *The Cambridgeshire Fens*

Bigmore P, *The Bedfordshire and Huntingdonshire Landscape*

Bloom A, *The Farm on the Fen*

Day JWA, *History of the Fens*

Dring WE, *The Fenland Story*

Dring WE, *The Fen and the Furrow*

Farrar Rev CF, *Ouse's Silent Tide*

Gray P, *The Washlanders*

90 Goodwin Sir HG, *Fenland: Its Ancient Past and Uncertain Future*

Heathcote JM, *Reminiscences of Fen and Mere*

Humphreys J, *Days and Nights on Hunter's Fen*

James A, *Memories of a Fen Tiger*

Leeming MA, *History of Food from Manna to Microwave*

Marshall S, *Fenland Chronicle*

Mee A, Ed, *The Counties of Bedford and Huntingdon*

Morris J, *History from the Sources; Domesday Book Huntingdonshire*

Norris HE, *Hunts County Sketches.*

Newell J, *The Holywell Story*

Page W, Ed, *The Victoria County History* Vols 1 and 2

Randell A, *Sixty Years a Fenman*

Rivington RT, *Punts and Punting*

Rotary Club of Ely, *The Battle of the Banks*

Storey EA, *Portrait of a Fen Country*

Tebbutt CF, *Huntingdonshire Folklore*

Tebbutt CF, *History of Bluntisham and Earith*

Wickes MA, *History of Huntingdonshire*

Woodger A, *An Introduction to Ancient Huntingdonshire*

OTHER SOURCES OF REFERENCE

Census Returns: 1841, 1851, 1861, 1871, 1891

Hunts County Guardian

Hunts County News

Hunts Post

Kelly's Directories

Looking Back on a Village 1875-1975, Holywell-cum-Needingworth School

River and Great Ouse Catchment Report on the Floods April 1947

Inskipp Ladds' File on Holywell and Needingworth-Norris Museum

Motorboats Monthly Great Ouse and Nene Guide

Oyster catcher

ABOUT THE AUTHOR

Nita Luxford was born in the north east of England and spent her early life in Durham City. Trained as an infants' teacher, she moved to St Ives, Huntingdonshire, in the early 1960s. With her husband, Brian, she moved to Hemingford Grey after the birth of the first of their two sons.

In the early 1990s she took early retirement from teaching reading and writing in primary schools and worked as a private tutor and freelance journalist, contributing to such publications as *Country Talk*, *The Countrylover's Magazines*, *Country Origins*, *The Countryman* and *Cambridgeshire Journal*.

Nita Luxford beside the Great Ouse at Hemingford Grey

PICTURE CREDITS

The majority of pictures in this book are from the Metcalfe-Arnold family collection.

Philip Nixon supplied the photographs on pages 6 and 7.

The late J Slater supplied the photographs on pages 34, 73 and 74.

The pictures on pages 79, 80, 81, 82, 85, 86 and 87 (Dolly Arnold) are by the late J Freeman.

The photograph on page 23 is from Cannon Photographic.

The photograph on page 25 is from Gordon Wilmer.

The two pictures on page 89 are by Nita Luxford.

P Seamark supplied the illustration on page 10, LH Jones & Son Ltd produced the map on page 8, and Roger Watson and Joe Newell provided additional pictures.

The sketches are by Helen Fenton, David Lovegrove and Nita Luxford.